Rutherford B. Hayes

☆ ★ ☆

Rutherford B. Hayes

Steven Otfinoski

AMERICA'S
19TH
PRESIDENT

Children's Press®
A Division of Scholastic Inc.
New York / Toronto / London / Auckland / Sydney
Mexico City / New Delhi / Hong Kong
Danbury, Connecticut

Library of Congress Cataloging-in-Publication Data

Otfinoski, Steven.
    Rutherford B. Hayes / by Steven Otfinoski.
        p. cm. — (Encyclopedia of presidents. Second series)
        Summary: A biography of the nineteenth president of the United States,
with information on his childhood, family, political career, presidency,
and legacy.
Includes bibliographical references and index.
  ISBN 0-516-22866-8
    1. Hayes, Rutherford Birchard, 1822–1893—Juvenile literature. 2.
Presidents—United States—Biography—Juvenile literature. [1. Hayes,
Rutherford Birchard, 1822–1893. 2. Presidents.] I. Title. II. Series.
E682.O84 2003
973.8'3'092—dc22   2003015959

Contents

One   7
A Natural Leader

Two   21
The Test of War

Three   33
From Congress to the White House

Four   55
A Good President

Five   75
The Final Years

Six   89
Legacy

Presidential Fast Facts   96
First Lady Fast Facts   97
Timeline   98
Glossary   100
Further Reading   101
Places to Visit   102
Online Sites of Interest   103
Table of Presidents   104
Index   108

Chapter 1

Controversial Elections ————————

In November 2000, the United States experienced one of the closest presidential elections in its history. Democratic candidate Albert Gore received more popular votes than Republican candidate George W. Bush, but neither candidate won enough votes in the electoral college to become president. The election hinged on the vote in Florida, where the result was very close and there were charges of voting irregularities. Disputes about recounts of the vote in key counties were carried to the U.S. Supreme Court. Only days before the inauguration, the Court awarded Florida's vote and the election to George W. Bush in a highly controversial decision.

In 1876, 124 years earlier, a strangely similar presidential election took place. Democratic candidate Samuel J. Tilden received more popular votes than Republican candidate Rutherford B. Hayes, but neither candidate received a majority of votes in the electoral college. Voting results in four states—including Florida—were contested. A special Electoral Commission appointed by Congress made the final controversial decision. It awarded the electoral votes of all four contested states to Republican Rutherford B. Hayes, electing him president only days before the scheduled inauguration.

A cartoon after the election of 1876 shows candidates Samuel Tilden and "Ruthie Hayes" as children. Tilden complains, "Ruthie has my presidency and won't give it back."

Hayes entered the presidency under a cloud of resentment and suspicion. Yet he proved to be an able and popular president. Historians believe that he was one of the most successful presidents in the 40 years between Abraham Lincoln and Theodore Roosevelt.

Lonely Child, Industrious Youth ——————

Rutherford Birchard Hayes was born on October 4, 1822, in Delaware, Ohio, a small town about 15 miles (24 kilometers) from Columbus, the state capital. His father, Rutherford Hayes Jr., had grown up in Brattleboro, Vermont, and later became part-owner of a general store in nearby Dummerston. The War of 1812 caused serious economic hardship in the region, however, so Rutherford moved west to Ohio in 1817 with his wife, Sophia Birchard Hayes, and their two small children, Lorenzo and Sara. It was a wise move. Rutherford Hayes Jr. soon owned a successful store and productive farmland. A second daughter, Fanny, was born in 1820, but four-year-old Sara died the following year.

Then in July 1822, tragedy struck once again. One day when Rutherford Hayes was clearing a field on his land, he was overcome with fever. His condition worsened rapidly, and three days later he died. Sophia Hayes was left with two young children and was expecting the birth of a third. Rutherford Birchard Hayes was born in October.

The birthplace of Rutherford Hayes in Delaware, Ohio.

"Ruddy," as he was called, was not a strong infant. His mother did not expect him to survive through childhood. Yet when tragedy struck once again, it struck his older brother. In January 1825, when Rutherford was two, nine-year-old Lorenzo was ice-skating on a frozen pond. The ice was too thin. When it gave way, Lorenzo fell into the frigid water and drowned.

Rutherford and his five-year-old sister Fanny were the only surviving children. His mother concentrated most of her attention on her fragile son. She

A School in 1830

Years later, Hayes recalled one of the schools he attended in Delaware with his sister Fanny. At the time, their mother was away visiting relatives. Ruddy and Fanny were staying with the Wasson family, who lived nearby.

A district school was opened near our house and Mr. Wasson thought it best for us to go. The school was free to all and was crowded with scholars of all ages, from little folks of our own size up to young men grown. The school-master, Daniel Granger, was a little, thin, wiry, energetic Yankee, with black hair, sallow complexion, and piercing black eyes; and when excited appeared to us a demon of ferocity. He flogged great strapping fellows of twice his size, and talked savagely of making them "dance about like a parched pea," and throwing them through the walls of the schoolhouse. He threw a large jack-knife, carefully aimed so as just to miss, at the head of a boy who was whispering near me. All the younger scholars were horribly afraid of him. We thought our lives were in danger. We knew he would kill some of us. Fanny and I begged Mr. Wasson with many tears to take us out of school. But he knew Mr. Granger to be a kind-hearted little man [and] insisted on our going.

☆ ★ ☆

did not allow him to play outside or go to school with other children. Instead, she taught him at home. Ruddy grew extremely close to his big sister, who became his closest friend and his inspiration. He once called Fanny "the confidante of all my life."

The man who helped change Ruddy's life was Sardis Birchard, his mother's unmarried brother. For a time, Uncle Sardis moved into the house in Delaware and became a second father to Ruddy. Even after he moved away, Sardis Birchard took a deep interest in his young nephew. When the boy was seven, Sardis persuaded Ruddy's mother to let him have a normal childhood. For the first time, he was allowed to play with other children and go to school. Hayes blossomed. He was good at games, and he became an excellent student. In elementary school he became a champion speller at spelling bees. Years later, Hayes boasted heartily, "Not one in a thousand could spell me down!"

Sardis Birchard also helped pay for Fanny's and Ruddy's education. Before he turned 14, Ruddy Hayes entered Norwalk Academy in Norwalk, Ohio, nearly 90 miles (145 km) from home. The next year he attended the exclusive Isaac Webb's Preparatory School in far-off Middletown, Connecticut.

He returned to Ohio, and at 16, he entered Kenyon College, in Gambier, Ohio, which was barely 40 miles (64 km) from home, much closer than his earlier schools. There he made many friends, enjoyed playing sports, and was a good student. He often wrote letters home to his mother and sister. Like many college students, he complained about his professors and the hard work, but he was usually cheerful. He graduated in three years, ranked first in his class.

Hayes participated in debating and speaking societies at college. By the time he graduated, he decided that he would become a lawyer. For a year, he read law in Columbus, but was bored and unhappy. In 1843, he was admitted to the Harvard Law School in Cambridge, Massachusetts, where he studied with Judge Joseph Story, a justice of the U.S. Supreme Court. During his two years at Harvard, he often visited his Hayes relatives in Vermont.

Hayes continued to enjoy his studies, and he made many friends at Harvard Law whom he would meet again in his political career. In his journal, however, he was often critical of his own behavior. In one entry he wrote, "Trifling remarks, boyish conduct, etc., are among my crying sins. Mend, mend! . . . I am quite lame from scuffling, and all my fingers stiffened from playing ball. Pretty business for a law student."

Five Wasted Years

In 1845, Hayes completed his studies. He returned to Ohio and was licensed to practice as a lawyer. He was a few months short of his 23rd birthday. He might have begun practicing law at home in Delaware or a few miles away in Columbus. Instead, he decided to start out in Lower Sandusky, in northern Ohio, where his uncle Sardis Birchard had settled. Birchard was a successful businessman. He offered his nephew a place to live and connections to many important people in the town. Hayes formed a partnership with another young lawyer, Ralph Buckland, and began looking for business.

Lower Sandusky was a town struggling to become a city. It was the home of shipping businesses that used the Sandusky River to reach Lake Erie, only 20 miles (32 km) away, from which goods could be transported to other ports on the lake. As railroads grew in importance, the town was in danger of being left behind. Another problem was that it was often confused with the bigger city of Sandusky, not far away.

Hayes and his partner never succeeded in building a good law practice in the town. However, Hayes did provide an important service while he was there. In 1849, he petitioned the city to change its name from Lower Sandusky to Fremont, in honor of one of the heroes of the day, John Charles Frémont. Frémont was a famous adventurer and soldier who had surveyed large regions of the West. In 1847, during the U.S.-Mexican War, he helped organize a revolution against Mexico in California. The town fathers agreed with young Hayes and renamed the town.

Hayes finally decided to give up his practice in Fremont and try his skills in a larger city. He chose Cincinnati, in the far southwestern part of the state, then one of the most prosperous and promising cities in the region. It was a good move. "Oh! The waste of those five precious years!" he wrote a few years later.

Still, he never gave up his connection to Frémont the man or Fremont the town. A few years later, he would proudly campaign for John C. Frémont when he became the first presidential nominee of the Republican party. Still later, when Sardis Birchard died, Hayes inherited his uncle's estate in Fremont, Ohio, and he would live there in retirement. Today it is the home of the Rutherford B. Hayes Presidential Center.

Success in Cincinnati

Hayes arrived in the big city of Cincinnati on December 24, 1849, a few months after his 27th birthday. He took a new partner, John W. Herron, and started again to build a law practice. At first business was so slow that Hayes and his partner lived and slept in a corner of the office to save expenses.

Soon Hayes proved to be a talented defense lawyer. In 1852, he took three highly publicized murder cases. One case concerned Nancy Farrer, who was accused of poisoning several members of her family. There was little doubt that she had poisoned them, but it seemed clear that she was mentally ill. Hayes

Cincinnati in the 1850s was an important city on the Ohio River, a major center for business and trade.

argued that she was not guilty by reason of insanity. Although she was convicted in the original trial, Hayes appealed the case to higher courts. Finally, in 1854, the Ohio Supreme Court agreed that Nancy Farrer was insane. She was confined to a hospital for the mentally ill. Hayes gained admiring attention in the Cincinnati newspapers for his skillful defense in criminal trials. He received invitations to lecture at debating societies and clubs on important issues of the day. He spoke often about the death penalty, which he strongly opposed.

Lucy

Hayes did not devote all his time to the law. During his early years in Cincinnati, he was courting Lucy Webb. He had first met her years before when her family was visiting his hometown, but, he recalled later, "she was too young to fall in love with, so I didn't."

Lucy was the daughter of a doctor in Chillicothe, Ohio. Like Hayes, Lucy had suffered from the death of her father before she was old enough to remember him. By 1850, Lucy was a student at the Wesleyan Female College in Cincinnati. She graduated that year, and soon afterward she and Rutherford were engaged.

"[She has] a heart as true as steel," Hayes wrote in his diary. "Intellect she has too. . . . By George! I'm in love with her!"

Rutherford Hayes and Lucy Webb made a handsome couple on their wedding day.

The couple was married on December 30, 1852. Hayes was 30 and Lucy, 21. The following year, their first child, Birchard Hayes, was born.

The ambitious young lawyer was about to enter a new arena—politics.

Chapter 2

The Country Divides

As Rutherford Hayes was rising in the legal profession and beginning a family, the United States was beginning to break apart. In the North, sentiment against slavery was growing by leaps and bounds. *Abolitionists*, who demanded an immediate end to slavery, claimed that it was immoral. *Free-Soilers* were content to let slavery exist in the South but were opposed to letting it spread to any new states made from the western territories. In the South, resentment of northern crusaders grew, and many in the region rallied to the defense of slavery. They feared that the North, which was growing faster, would soon overwhelm the South in Congress and would restrict or even outlaw slavery. Southern leaders began to talk about *seceding*, withdrawing from the United States, to protect slavery and each state's rights to make its own laws.

In the meantime, leaders in the federal government worked feverishly to find compromises that would hold the country together. Their main aim was to keep the *Union*, the United States, together. These leaders opposed both the abolitionists in the North and the extreme defenders of slavery in the South. However, each compromise they made seemed to cause deeper anger and hostility between these two regions of the country.

In 1854, Congress passed the Kansas-Nebraska Act. Its main purpose was to prepare parts of the huge Nebraska Territory to gain admission as new states. It proposed to let residents of each new state decide by a vote whether to permit or forbid slavery. This new compromise brought a wave of political change in the North. Soon the people who opposed any spread of slavery got together to form the new Republican party. Rutherford Hayes soon joined the Republican party in Ohio. In 1856, he campaigned enthusiastically for its first candidate for president, John C. Frémont. Republicans did not yet have support in many parts of the country, however, and Frémont lost the election to Democrat James Buchanan.

The same year, Hayes lost one of the dearest people in his life. His sister, Fanny Hayes Platt, had married in 1839 and already had four children. In 1856, she died after giving birth to twins, who also died soon afterward. "Oh what a blow it is!" Hayes wrote in a letter. The sister who had encouraged and cared for him would not be there to enjoy his later successes.

Hayes looks directly at the camera in this early photographic portrait.

In 1858 the Cincinnati city *solicitor*, or attorney, died suddenly. The city council chose Hayes to complete his unfinished term. A year later, having performed well in the job, Hayes was elected to a two-year term as city solicitor. In the 1860 presidential election, Hayes campaigned for Republican nominee Abraham Lincoln, who was elected. When Hayes came up for reelection early in 1861, he was defeated by a huge protest vote against Lincoln and Republicans. Cincinnati was just across the Ohio River from the slave state of Kentucky, and residents feared that a Republican government would bring conflict and disrupt business in the region. They were right. The Civil War began soon afterward. Hayes hardly had time to regret his loss in the election. The 38-year-old lawyer soon enlisted and marched off to war.

A Valiant Officer

At age 38, Hayes could have stayed out of the fighting. Not only was he a prominent lawyer and civic leader, he had two young children (Birchard, born in 1853, and James, born in 1856). Lucy would soon give birth to a third son. Hayes found staying home unthinkable. "I would prefer to go into [the war] if I knew I was to die," he wrote, "rather than to live through and after it without taking any part in it."

Hayes enlisted on April 20, eight days after the war began. Early in June he received the rank of major in the 23rd Ohio Volunteer Infantry. After six weeks

Hayes was first wounded at the Battle of Cheat Mountain in present-day West Virginia. Before the fighting ended in 1865, he had been wounded four times.

of training, the 23rd Ohio was sent to western Virginia, where they would do most of their fighting over the next four years. They saw their first action in a Union victory at Cheat Mountain Pass in September. Hayes led an attack on a hill held by Confederates and drove them off of it. For his bravery, he was promoted to lieutenant colonel.

In February 1862, Hayes returned home on leave. He saw his youngest son, Joseph, born in December 1861, for the first time. The older children scarcely recognized their father. He had not shaved for six months, and returned with full beard. They would get used to his changed appearance, however. Hayes kept his beard for the rest of his life.

That summer, Hayes and the 23rd Ohio were sent to Maryland to help defend against an attack by Robert E. Lee's Confederate army. On September 14, Hayes led an attack on Confederate positions at South Mountain. He was struck by a musket ball which broke his left arm. Stranded in no-man's-land between the two fighting forces, he ignored his vulnerable position and continued to shout orders to his men, inspiring them onward. At a field hospital, he was treated by the unit's doctor, Joseph Webb, Lucy Hayes's brother. Soon afterward, Lucy arrived from Ohio to help nurse her husband back to health. She also tended other wounded soldiers there. Hayes went home with Lucy to Ohio to recuperate and did not return to duty for ten weeks. During his leave, he was promoted to full colonel.

During the spring and summer of 1863, Lucy and the children paid long visits to Hayes while his unit was stationed at Camp Reynolds and Camp White in West Virginia. This region, formerly part of Virginia, had remained loyal to the Union, and in 1863, it was admitted as a state. During one of these family visits, young Joseph Hayes, only 18 months old, came down with dysentery and died.

Even though Hayes had no military training before joining the army, he proved himself to be a skilled commander. By 1864, the 23rd Ohio was a battle-tested unit, and Hayes had been entrusted with command of a battalion which included the 23rd. That summer, a Confederate army led by Jubal Early marched through the Great Valley of Virginia and into Union territory in Maryland. Hayes's battalion became part

Fast Facts
THE CIVIL WAR

Who: The United States (the Union, or the North) against the Confederate States of America, made up of southern states that had seceded from the Union.

When: April 12, 1861–May 1865

Why: Southern states, believing the election of Abraham Lincoln threatened states' rights and slavery, seceded from the United States and fought for their independence. The North fought to restore the southern states to the Union, and later to end slavery.

Where: States along the border between the Union and the Confederacy, especially Virginia and Tennessee. Confederate forces had some early successes, but were overcome by the Union's superior resources. Major northern victories came at Gettysburg, Pennsylvania, and Vicksburg, Mississippi (both July 1863); Atlanta, Georgia (September 1864); and Petersburg and Richmond, Virginia (both April 1865).

Outcome: The Confederate Army of Northern Virginia surrendered to Union forces April 9, 1865, ending the major fighting. The victorious North passed legislation that abolished slavery, gave civil rights to former slaves, and put defeated states under military rule. Efforts to reconstruct the South continued until 1877.

of the Army of the Shenandoah, which had the job of driving the Confederates south.

In September, Hayes was given command the Second Division in the army and saw action in a series of battles, as the Confederates were driven south and west through the Great Valley. On October 19, at Cedar Creek, near

Presidents of the Civil War

Five of six future presidents between 1869 and 1901 proved their ability to lead during the Civil War. All five were born in Ohio. The most prominent was Ulysses S. Grant. A graduate of the U.S. Military Academy, he became the North's most effective general. He was appointed General in Chief of all Union armies in 1864 and helped plan the strategy that finally won the war.

James A. Garfield, like Hayes, first commanded a troop of Ohio volunteers. He fought bravely at several major battles, including Shiloh and Chickamauga. Benjamin Harrison took part in the Union campaign against Atlanta, Georgia. Finally, William McKinley enlisted as a lowly private and served under Hayes in the 23rd Ohio Volunteers. By the end of the war, still only 22 years old, McKinley was promoted to major.

Only one president during the period did not serve in the Civil War. Grover Cleveland was supporting his widowed mother and his younger brothers and sisters. When he was drafted, he paid for a substitute to take his place, a common practice at the time.

☆☆☆

Strasburg, Virginia, Early's troops launched a surprise attack against Hayes's division. In the intense fighting, his horse was shot and killed, and Hayes himself was hit and knocked unconscious. When he revived, he found another horse and resumed command. General Philip Sheridan, the commander of the army, helped regroup Union forces, and they counterattacked, achieving a major victory. Sheridan promoted Hayes to *brevet* (temporary) major general for his bravery and leadership.

A Soldier in Congress

Hayes's wartime exploits made him a hero back home in Ohio. Cincinnati Republicans were eager to have him run for a congressional seat. He was offered the nomination in 1862 and refused it, but in 1864, he accepted with the understanding that he would not return to Ohio to campaign. "I have other business just now," he wrote in a letter. "An officer fit for duty who at this crisis would abandon his post to electioneer for a seat in Congress ought to be scalped."

Hayes's military successes were the best campaigning he could have done. He easily won the election in October 1864. He resigned from the army on June 8, 1865, about two months after the surrender of Confederate general Robert E. Lee at Appomattox Court House, Virginia. Hayes had been wounded

General Ulysses S. Grant (left) receives the surrender of General Robert E. Lee's Confederate Army in 1865. Less than four years later, Grant was elected president.

four times and had four horses shot out from under him. He had risen from major to brevet major general in four years of war. In December 1865, he took his seat in Congress and entered into a new struggle—to rebuild a war-torn nation.

Junior Congressman ————————————

In April 1865, only days after the Confederate surrender, Abraham Lincoln was assassinated. This brought the vice president, Andrew Johnson, to the White House. Johnson, a Democrat from Tennessee, wanted to restore southern states to the Union quickly, and was willing to let them establish new state governments on their own. Showing some of the same intensity he had shown on the battlefield, Hayes joined the Radical Republicans, who opposed the president. They insisted that Confederate states must be "reconstructed" and must agree to grant the rights of citizenship to African Americans before they could be brought back into the Union.

Hayes was also appointed chairman of a joint House-Senate committee on the Library of Congress. He and his colleagues recommended congressional actions that would make the library more accessible to all citizens.

Rutherford Hayes in uniform near the end of the Civil War. He has grown a beard, which he would wear for the rest of his life.

Governor of Ohio

Hayes won a second term in Congress in 1866, but he missed his family. When Congress was in session, he lived in Washington, while they stayed home in Cincinnati. In 1867, he resigned his seat in Congress to run for governor of Ohio. In a hotly contested battle against the strong Democratic party in the state, Hayes managed to win the governorship by a tiny margin—only 3,000 votes. He took office early in 1868.

That spring, the House of Representatives *impeached* President Andrew Johnson, accusing him of high crimes and misdemeanors as president. Radical Republicans, including some friends of Hayes, served as prosecutors in Johnson's trial. After weeks of testimony, the Senate, which served as the jury, failed to convict Johnson by one vote.

In the fall, General of the Army Ulysses S. Grant was the Republican nominee for president to replace Johnson. Grant won with the support of the Radical Republicans. The new administration campaigned for states to ratify the Fifteenth Amendment to the Constitution, guaranteeing the right of African Americans to vote. The amendment had already been passed by Congress, but required ratification by three-fourths of the states to take effect.

As governor, Hayes used his power and the reputation of his office to encourage ratification of the amendment in Ohio. In the southern part of the state, it was very unpopular, but Hayes's Republican administration succeeded in gaining ratification in a very close vote. He later proposed an amendment to the Ohio state constitution guaranteeing African Americans' voting rights, but failed to gain its passage.

Hayes's stand on voting rights weakened his party in Ohio, and Democrats won majorities in the state legislature in 1869. Even so, Hayes himself remained popular and was reelected that fall. During his second term, he helped to establish the state's first public institution of higher learning. It was called the Ohio Agricultural and Mechanical College and would grow to become Ohio State University, one of the nation's largest and most admired state universities.

Ohio was becoming an important mining and manufacturing center during Hayes's years as governor. Workers in mines and factories and on the railroads worked long hours in very dangerous conditions. There were many accidents causing death and injury. Hayes helped establish state safety regulations for workers. Recalling his years as a defense lawyer, he also led the fight for reform of prisons and mental hospitals.

Hayes gained a strong reputation for appointing highly qualified men to state positions. Other political leaders gave jobs to those they owed favors to. Hayes looked for appointees who had the skills and experience to do a good job.

The broad, flat expanse of Columbus, the capital of Ohio, where Hayes served as a legislator and as governor. The State House is at the left.

His interest in reforming the way government workers are chosen continued into his presidency.

As his second term came near its end in 1871, Hayes refused to break tradition and run for a third term. He left office in early 1872, but Republican leaders persuaded him to run for Congress again in 1872. It was a difficult election for Republicans in southern Ohio, where the Democratic party had grown stronger. Hayes lost the election. Republicans were stronger in the state as a whole. President Grant, running for reelection, managed to carry the state.

Grant offered Hayes the position of assistant U.S. treasurer in Cincinnati, but Hayes refused the appointment. His uncle Sardis Birchard was old and ill and had invited the Hayes family to live on his estate, Spiegel Grove, in Fremont. Hayes, Lucy, and their younger children moved to Fremont. Hayes helped Birchard with his business affairs and the family helped care for him during his last illness. He died in January 1874, leaving Spiegel Grove to his nephew. It would be the permanent home of Rutherford and Lucy Hayes for the rest of their lives.

Now in his early 50s, Hayes spent his days reading books, tending to his spacious grounds, and managing his uncle's real estate holdings. Much as he enjoyed his early retirement, however, he still burned with political ambition.

The Race for President

By 1875, the Republican party in Ohio was in trouble. The state was governed by a Democratic governor and legislature. Once again, Ohio Republicans called on Hayes, urging him to run again for governor. He accepted their invitation. He was already looking beyond Ohio to possible national office. "Several suggest that if elected Governor now, I will stand well for the Presidency next year," he wrote in his diary. "How wild! What a queer lot we are becoming! Nobody is out of the reach of that mania."

Meanwhile, the administration of President Grant in Washington was in shambles. In 1873, a severe depression hit the country, causing widespread losses and suffering. Banks closed, prices dropped, workers lost their jobs, and farmers could not sell their crops. Grant was under great pressure to issue more paper money to get the economy started again. Like most Republicans, he resisted issuing paper money that could not be backed by gold. Many in the nation blamed his administration for their troubles. In 1874, voters took action by electing Democratic majorities in the House and Senate.

Grant was also being hurt by revelations of corruption in his administration. Although nearly everyone believed that he was personally honest, many of the government officers he appointed were making themselves rich.

Corruption of the Grant Presidency

President Grant seemed to have a talent for appointing men who knew how to enrich themselves by selling government favors. His two vice presidents, Schuyler Colfax and Henry Wilson, were both implicated in the Crédit Mobilier scandal, which occurred even before Grant took office. They received free stock in the company, which built railroads. In return for the valuable stock, the company's owners expected favors for the railroads from the government.

In 1869, two greedy investors even involved a member of Grant's family. Jay Gould and Jim Fisk made friends with Abel Corbin, who was married to Grant's sister. They used him to learn about government plans for selling gold and used the knowledge to make huge profits. When Grant learned of their scheme, he changed government policy, ending the scheme. Hundreds of small investors were ruined by the change, however.

Another group was accepting bribes from the "Whiskey Ring," a group of liquor manufacturers. In return for the bribes, these officials agreed not to collect government taxes on the whiskey, allowing the manufacturers to make large profits. Everyone benefited except the government.

Still other members of the government made money by selling government appointments. A person wanting a particular position might pay a large amount before appointment, or he might agree to pay a percentage of his salary for as long as he held his position.

By 1876 these practices had overwhelmed Grant's government. He hoped to run for a third term as president, but both Republicans and Democrats were looking for a candidate who could "clean up the mess" in Washington.

☆ ☆ ☆

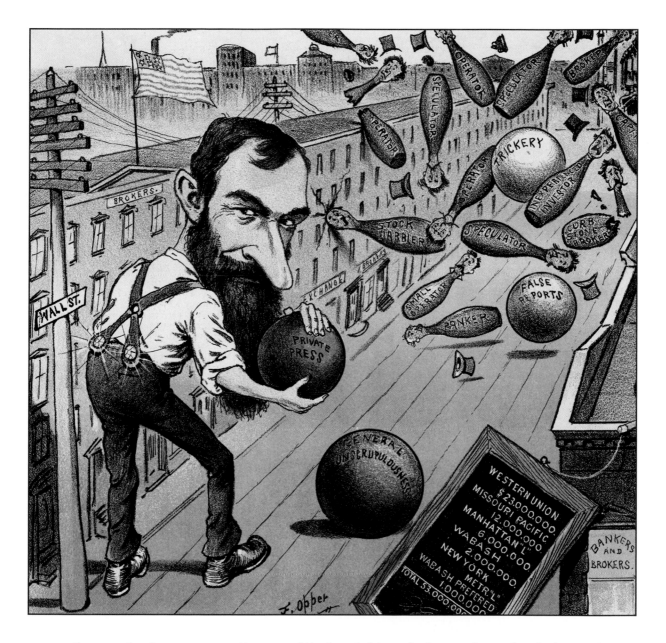

This cartoon shows businessman Jay Gould as a successful bowler. Each of the pins has the name of a group he took advantage of. He nearly cornered the market for gold in 1869, with help from friends and appointees of Grant.

In 1875, Hayes was elected to his third term as governor. Almost immediately, he was being mentioned as a possible candidate for president in 1876. Even though the voters had elected Republican presidents in each of the last four elections, economic depression and the corruption in the Grant administration convinced many voters that it was time for a change. The Republican party itself had split into factions. The group that called itself the Stalwarts strongly supported President Grant for a third term. The reform faction was strongly opposed to Grant. In the last presidential election, they had broken with the Republican party and nominated their own candidate to run against him. In the middle were the moderates, who hoped to keep the party together.

The leading candidate for president was James G. Blaine, a former congressional leader and a moderate. Yet he had been charged with making a personal profit in one of the scandals of the Grant government. The Stalwarts, led by the powerful senator from New York, Roscoe Conkling, continued to hold out for Grant. Reform Republicans backed Benjamin Bristow of Kentucky. He had gained support by investigating and exposing corruption in the Treasury Department, but he was despised by the Stalwarts.

Following the fashion of the time, Hayes did not participate directly in his campaign for the nomination, but he had the support of some experienced political operators. They presented Hayes as a perfect candidate to unite the party.

This cartoon shows Grant near the end of his second term, weighed down with scandals and failures. The barking dogs are newspapers critical of his actions.

The Centennial Exhibition

Besides being an election year, 1876 was the 100th birthday of the United States. A grand Centennial Exhibition was held in Philadelphia from May to November. The exhibition spread over 285 acres (115 hectares) and contained more than 200 buildings specially built for the occasion. Exhibitions celebrated the arts, sciences, agriculture, and industry in the United States and around the world. The huge Machinery Hall was among the most popular gathering places. At its center was the awesome Corliss engine, a giant steam engine that provided power for dozens of mechanical exhibits in the hall.

The Hall of Machinery at the exposition (above). Three newspapers printed their editions on presses in the hall, and other machines sawed logs, printed wallpaper, and stitched up ready-made clothes. Power for these activities was generated by the huge Corliss engine (right), which became a major attraction itself.

More than 30 nations sponsored exhibits, and millions of visitors came to Philadelphia to enjoy the exhibition's many wonders. Among the visitors were world leaders, President Grant, and the Hayes family. The admission price was 50 cents. The Centennial Exhibition was the first world's fair held in the United States, and it set a model for many world's fairs in the years to come. "It is impossible to describe [the fair]," wrote one breathless reporter. "Nothing but seeing it with your own eyes can give you any conception of its magnitude."

★ ★ ☆

Since he had not been involved in national politics for nearly ten years, he had made fewer enemies than other candidates. He kept up friendships with members of all the Republican factions. In addition, his record as governor of Ohio appealed to reformers. There was no suggestion that he had been involved in any government corruption.

The 1876 Republican convention was held in Cincinnati, which had long been Hayes's hometown. Ohioans who supported him helped organize the convention, and local crowds could be counted on to cheer loudly for him. On the first day, supporters gave dramatic nominating speeches for each major candidate. The speech for Blaine set off a long, enthusiastic demonstration for his nomination. Just when it seemed that Blaine might be nominated on the first *ballot* (round of voting), the lights went out, ending business until the next day.

During the night, Hayes's supporters made several important bargains with supporters of other candidates. When the first ballot was held, Blaine had the most votes, but was far short of the number needed for nomination. In each following ballot, he lost votes, and Hayes gained. Finally, on the seventh ballot, Republicans chose Rutherford B. Hayes. William A. Wheeler, a New York congressman, was later nominated as vice president.

Two weeks later, the Democratic convention met in St. Louis. It selected the governor of New York, Samuel J. Tilden, as its candidate. Tilden had a strong record as a reformer in his home state. He campaigned against the corruption of the Grant administration in Washington, and pledged to end the harsh Republican policy of using federal troops to police several southern states.

Hayes was also a strong reform candidate. He pledged to create a civil service system for appointing many federal workers, which would help end the sale of jobs that helped corrupt government operations. The Republicans also pointed out that their party had led the crusade to save the Union in the Civil War, while Democrats were still identified with the rebellious South and slavery.

With the two sides so evenly matched, the election was sure to be close. Two weeks before election day, Hayes wrote in his diary, "Another danger is imminent: a contested result. And we have no such means for its decision as ought to be provided by law. This must be attended to hereafter. . . . If a contest comes now it may lead to a conflict of arms." His fears soon proved to be justified.

A Disputed Election —————————————

The Democrats turned out in full force on election day. By evening, Hayes was convinced he had lost. The final popular vote backed that belief: Tilden had 4,284,020 votes to Hayes's 4,036,572—a margin of nearly 250,000. Tilden had also carried states that gave him 184 electoral votes, only one short of the majority he needed for election.

The Republicans did not concede, however. Twenty electoral votes were still contested, one in Oregon and the remaining 19 in the states of Florida, South Carolina, and Louisiana. In each of these three states, Republicans claimed that white Democrats had used unfair means (including terror) to keep African Americans from voting. Democrats claimed that Republicans had stuffed the ballot boxes with extra Republican votes and tampered with the vote count. A Republican victory was a long shot. The party needed every disputed electoral vote to win. The Democrats needed only a single disputed electoral vote to elect their candidate.

The election was thrown into the House of Representatives, but it could not decide who should judge votes in the disputed states. December came and went and still the election was not decided. Tempers flared, and angry voters demonstrated for their candidates. Someone fired a bullet through Hayes's porch window while the family was eating dinner. Mobs of angry Democrats marched through towns and cities chanting "Tilden or Blood!" Could the nation be on the brink of a second civil war?

President Grant urged the nation to remain calm. The two candidates urged Congress to find a peaceful solution. On January 29, 1877, Congress set up an Electoral Commission consisting of five senators, five representatives, and five justices of the Supreme Court. There were seven Republicans and seven Democrats. The 15th member, Justice David Davis, was pledged to be nonpartisan.

The U.S. Congress meets to receive the results of the vote for president in the electoral college. Three states sent two sets of results, making it impossible to decide who had been elected. The Congress appointed a 15-member Electoral Commission to decide.

Samuel J. Tilden

Samuel Tilden (1814–1886) believed until his death that he was cheated out of the presidency. He was born in New Lebanon, New York, in 1814, and studied law in New York City. He was elected to the New York State Assembly as a Democrat, and became a leader of the antislavery Democrats who supported the Free-Soil party. Later, he made a fortune as a corporate lawyer, working mostly for major railroads.

After the Civil War, as state Democratic chairman, he joined Republicans in opposing the corrupt Democratic machine in New York City. Known as the Tweed Ring, it was named after its leader, William "Boss" Tweed. Largely through Tilden's efforts, the ring was broken in 1871, and Tweed was later convicted and sent to prison. Thanks to his reputation as a reformer, Tilden was elected governor of New York in 1874, the year before Hayes was elected to a third term as governor of Ohio.

Samuel J. Tilden, Democratic governor of New York, won more popular votes than Hayes in the 1876 election and believed he deserved to be president.

Although embittered by his experience in the contested 1876 election, Tilden remained a benefactor of the people to the end. On his death in 1886, Tilden bequeathed his wealth to a trust that helped establish the New York Public Library.

Before the commission could meet, however, Justice Davis was elected to the U.S. Senate by Democrats in the Illinois legislature. They hoped that his election would influence him to lean toward Tilden. Instead, Davis resigned from the commission. Justice Joseph Bradley, a Republican appointed to the Supreme Court by Grant, was named in his place.

When the commission met to consider the disputes in each state, the seven Republicans voted for Hayes and the seven Democrats voted for Tilden. Bradley, with the deciding vote, voted each time for Hayes. Hayes gained all 20 disputed electoral votes, and was elected by a vote of 185 to 184. Democrats were stunned. They threatened to vote against the Electoral Commission's decision in the House, where they held a majority. As March 5, inauguration day, drew nearer, it seemed the country might be without a president.

Finally, in private meetings, Democrats and Republicans came to an understanding. Harsh military rule in some southern states had been losing public support for years as violence continued with no end in sight. Republicans agreed that if Democrats would agree not to question the decision of the Electoral Commission, the new Republican administration would withdraw federal troops from the states they were still policing. Early on Friday, March 2, 1877, only three days before the scheduled inauguration, Rutherford B. Hayes was declared the next president.

The Electoral Commission (above) meets to settle the disputed election. A gun and a threatening message (right) express the nation's fear of violence when the result is announced.

The disputed and divisive election came to an end. Fearful of further demonstrations, leaders in Washington insisted that Hayes take the oath of office the following day, March 3. Hayes repeated the oath at the inaugural ceremony on Monday, March 5.

Chapter 4

A Good President

"Ruther-fraud"

The long, disruptive election caused President Hayes's first days in the White House to be anything but pleasant. The Democratic newspapers referred to him as "Ruther-fraud B. Hayes" and "His Fraudulency." After the inauguration ceremony, Ohio Republican James A. Garfield wrote in his diary, "There were many indications of relief and joy that no accident had occurred on the [parade] route, for there were apprehensions of assassination." There were no attempts to assassinate Hayes, but Garfield himself would be the victim of an assassin only four years later.

Rebuilding the South

Hayes set out to prove that he was worthy of being president. His first major act was to withdraw remaining federal troops from the South.

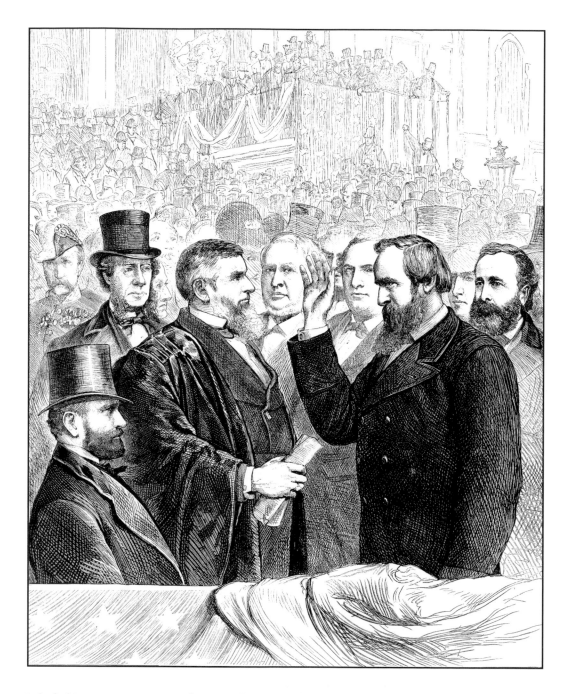

Rutherford B. Hayes is sworn in as president on March 5, 1877. At the lower left is retiring president Ulysses S. Grant.

That meant ending military occupation in the states of South Carolina and Louisiana. Removing the troops may have been a part of the agreement made between Republicans and Democrats to end the election dispute. Whether it was or not, Hayes believed that ending the military occupation was good policy.

After the Civil War, Hayes had been a strong supporter of Reconstruction and had favored sending federal troops to the South to protect the rights of African Americans. By 1877, however, twelve years had passed, and the troops still occupied two southern states. Deep divisions between southern whites and African Americans continued to cause unrest and violence. Hayes shared the views of many people in both the North and South that the military Reconstruction plan was not working. It was time for a new approach.

Hayes made it clear that he would not abandon the South. He wanted the region to become a strong and equal partner with the North. He urged Congress to begin a major program to rebuild and repair war damage in the South. Many Republicans opposed such help, but Hayes managed to gain federal support for some improvements in southern bridges, roads, and canals. Southern Democrats praised the new president, calling him "the greatest Southerner of the day." However, they refused his pleas to grant civil rights to African Americans. In fact, southern states began to pass laws that excluded African Americans, separating them from whites even in public places and obstructing their right to vote or participate in politics. This pattern of *segregation* continued without serious challenge for more than 50 years.

Ending the Spoils System

Hayes had pledged during the campaign to end the spoils system. In this system, elected officials filled government positions with their party's supporters, whether or not they were qualified for the jobs. Hayes knew that Republicans and Democrats alike would oppose ending the system.

As president, Hayes set an important example by appointing candidates who were well qualified to important positions. He shocked many northerners by naming David Key as postmaster general. Key was a former senator and an able man, but he was a southerner and a former lieutenant colonel in the Confederate army. Hayes appointed Carl Schurz to be secretary of the interior. A leading reformer and an outspoken critic of former president Grant, Schurz was a controversial appointee, but was one of the most brilliant men in the party. As secretary of the interior, he was an early supporter of preserving forests on federal lands, and he was also a strong supporter of ending the spoils system. Other top appointments included William M. Evarts as secretary of state and John Sherman as secretary of the treasury.

Carl Schurz

Carl Schurz (1829–1906) was a writer and reformer who became an important leader in the Republican party. He was born in Germany and fought as a young man in a failed revolution to establish a democratic government there. He fled to Britain, then to the United States. In 1855, he settled in Wisconsin, where there was a large German American population. He became a lawyer and an early member of the Republican party. In 1860, he was an important leader in the campaign to elect Abraham Lincoln to the presidency.

Carl Schurz, a leading Republican reformer, had been a general in the Civil War and a senator from Missouri. He served as Hayes's secretary of the interior and advised on many government reforms.

During the Civil War, Schurz entered the army and rose to the rank of major general. He commanded divisions at Second Bull Run, Chancellorsville, and Chattanooga. After the war, he became a prominent newspaper correspondent. In 1868, he moved to Missouri, where he supported Grant for president. He was elected to the U.S. Senate in 1869. Four years later, Senator Schurz helped organize the Liberal Republicans, who broke away from the Republican party and campaigned unsuccessfully against Grant's run for reelection. In 1876, Schurz supported Hayes for president, and was appointed to the cabinet. In addition to serving as secretary of the interior, he helped prepare a plan for civil service examinations to reform government hiring.

After Hayes left the presidency, Schurz became editor of the *New York Evening Post* and remained an important figure in the Republican party. He died in 1906.

☆ ★ ☆

Then Hayes went a step further by removing federal officials he believed to be corrupt. The New York Custom House was one of the most important federal offices in the country. The duties it collected on goods passing through New York harbor made up more than half of the federal government's income. The leading officer of the custom house, with the title Collector of the Port of New York, was Chester A. Arthur. Arthur was a prominent New York Republican who had been appointed through the efforts of Republican senator Roscoe Conkling. Only loyal Republicans were appointed to work in the Custom House, and it was generally believed that appointees were required to return part of their salaries to their bosses.

In 1877, Hayes risked the anger of his own party by removing Arthur from the Custom House and appointing a reformer in his place. Senator Conkling persuaded the Senate not to approve the new candidate. This preserved the custom called "senatorial courtesy," under which Republican senators had the right to approve appointments of federal officials in their own states. Hayes then suspended Arthur and persuaded the Senate to uphold his action. It was a major victory over the spoils system. Hayes also issued executive orders providing that government appointees could not be "assessed" contributions to political campaigns and that appointed federal officials could not "take part in the management of political organizations, caucuses, conventions, or election campaigns."

Chester Alan Arthur

Chester Alan Arthur (1829–1886) was born in Vermont, but studied law in New York and became a prominent attorney in New York City. As a close associate of Senator Roscoe Conkling, Arthur became a power in the New York Republican party. He was named head of the New York Custom House in 1871. It employed hundreds of workers chosen through the spoils system. As the director, Arthur may not have profited from the system himself, but he did little to change things. President Hayes began a campaign to remove Arthur in 1877 and suspended him from the office in 1878.

Chester A. Arthur was suspended from his position as director of the U.S. Custom House in New York by President Hayes, creating a serious split in the Republican party.

Two years later, Arthur became the Republican nominee for vice president, running with presidential nominee James Garfield. They won the election. Then in July 1881, four months after he took office, President Garfield was shot by an assassin. He died in September, and Arthur became president. Republicans feared that Arthur would reinstate the old spoils system. Instead, Arthur threw his support behind reform. On January 16, 1883, he signed the Pendleton Civil Service Act, a major step toward ending the spoils system in the federal government. Arthur left office in 1885 and died the following year in New York.

☆ ☆ ☆

The Economy

When Hayes entered office, the country was still recovering from an economic depression that began in 1873. In addition, the government was still facing the problem of paying off large debts taken on during the Civil War.

During the war, the U.S. Treasury had issued millions of "greenbacks," paper money that was not backed by gold. It promised that it would redeem the greenbacks with gold after January 1, 1879. As that date approached the government was struggling to buy enough gold to redeem all the bills. The Democratic-led Congress favored a "cheap money" policy, urging that the bills be redeemed for silver (which was more plentiful) rather than gold. Hayes *vetoed*, or refused to sign into law, two bills that called for free coinage of silver. He was convinced that a currency based on the gold standard would put the economy back on an even keel after years of economic uncertainty. He wrote that the silver bills would "launch the country on the dangerous sea of unlimited and irredeemable paper currency."

Congress came back with the revised Bland-Allison bill in 1878, which called for a more conservative coinage of silver. Hayes vetoed that bill, too. This time, Congress *overrode* his veto, passing it by two-thirds majorities in both the House and Senate, and the bill became law. It was a bitter personal defeat for the president.

The Great Railroad Strike of 1877 ———

Perhaps the most serious crisis of Hayes's presidency occurred in July 1877, when he had been in office only four months. Because business was still slow, major railroad companies announced that their workers would receive stiff cuts in pay.

Members of the Brotherhood of Locomotive Engineers in Martinsburg, West Virginia, walked off their jobs in protest. The railroad hired replacement workers to keep the railroad running, but the strikers interfered, threatening the new workers and damaging railroad equipment. The governor of West Virginia called out the state militia to keep order. The railroad strike quickly spread to Maryland, Pennsylvania, Illinois, and other states. Clashes between strikers and police and militia led to more than 60 deaths and millions of dollars in property damage. The governors of the first four states involved urged President Hayes to do something. He finally sent in federal troops to restore order. The troops were told not to fire on strikers except to protect themselves. The Great Railroad Strike of 1877 soon came to an end.

Hayes tried to strike a balance between the railroads' management and their workers. Still, strikers complained bitterly that he had interfered to protect the railroads and break their strike. He wrote in his diary, "Can't something [be]

Above, strikers burn the Union Depot in Pittsburgh during the railroad strike of 1877. At right, National Guardsmen fire on demonstrating strikers in Baltimore, Maryland.

done by education of the strikers, by judicious control of the capitalists, by wise general policy to end or diminish the evil?"

Rutherford the Rover

With continuing unrest in the South and labor conflict in the North, the people of the United States looked to the West for encouragement. The transcontinental railroad had been completed in 1869, and it allowed thousands to travel across the country to find new homes and opportunities. Hayes felt the need to see the growing West and let its residents see their president. In September 1880, he became the first president to travel to the Pacific, touring California and Oregon. Along with Lucy, two of his sons, and his niece Laura, Hayes visited Yosemite Valley in California, and the cities of Los Angeles, San Francisco, and Portland.

The president was welcomed warmly wherever he went and seemed to enjoy his visit. Back east, however, the press criticized him for spending so much time away from Washington. Newspaper editors nicknamed him "Rutherford the Rover."

Hayes's trips around the country were not simply leisure pursuits. They allowed him to view the country's problems and successes up close. After seeing the poverty of a number of Native Americans on Indian reservations, he worked to improve reservation life. In California, he heard complaints about Chinese

Hayes was the first president to visit the states on the Pacific coast. He and his family toured the Yosemite Valley to see the spectacular mountains and waterfalls.

immigrants taking over available jobs. When he returned to Washington, Congress presented Hayes with a bill to end all immigration from China. He vetoed the bill, which he believed would cause serious diplomatic problems with China. Instead, he sent a special envoy to China to negotiate a reduction in immigration to the United States in return for more trade between the countries.

William Almon Wheeler

"Who is Wheeler?" Hayes wrote his wife when he learned who had been nominated for vice president. Like many earlier vice presidents, William Almon Wheeler of New York was nominated to help win his home state in the presidential election. He served quietly, then retired without making a strong impression on his party or the country.

William Wheeler (1819–1887) was born in Malone, New York. When he was eight, Wheeler's father died. Wheeler had to work his way through school and studied law with a local lawyer. He was elected to the New York legislature in 1850 and to the state senate in 1858, then served terms in the U.S. Congress (1861–1863, and 1869–1877). In 1873 he voted against a 50 percent pay raise for Congress. When the raise was passed, Wheeler returned $5,000 in back pay to the U.S. Treasury.

Few vice presidents were as lonely and miserable as Wheeler. His wife died three months before he was nominated for vice president, and he had no other immediate family. The Hayes family adopted him, and he spent many pleasant evenings as a member of their extended family at the White House. When his term ended, he returned to Malone, where he died six years later, in 1887.

★ ★ ☆

Family Values

The Hayes family was affectionate and close-knit. When Rutherford and Lucy Hayes moved to the White House, Webb Hayes served as his father's personal secretary. Two sons, Birchard and Ruddy, were away at college. The younger children, Fanny and Scott, had the run of the White House. The family gathered each morning to say prayers together. Many evenings, they gathered around the parlor piano to listen to music and sing songs and hymns. Visitors were warmly invited to join them.

Late in 1877, Rutherford and Lucy Hayes celebrated their 25th wedding anniversary, welcoming the minister who married them in Cincinnati in 1852. The following year, Hayes was pleased to serve as host to the wedding of Emily Platt, his beloved sister's daughter.

The President and Congress

An important theme of Hayes's presidency was his long battle with Congress. In the years before he came to office, Congress had gained great power at the expense of the president. During Andrew Johnson's term, it passed dozens of bills over the president's veto, including a law that restricted the president's power to dismiss or appoint members of his own cabinet. Late in Johnson's term, Congress impeached Johnson, accusing him of defying laws that it had passed. Johnson

Lucy Ware Webb Hayes

Lucy Hayes (1831–1889) provided great support for her husband, but also fought for support for her own views. The first president's wife to graduate from college, Lucy had strongly supported ending slavery and granting more rights to women in her younger days.

During her years in the White House, Lucy did not speak publicly on these issues, but she may have spoken privately to her husband. "Mrs. Hayes may not have much influence with Congress," he once said, "but she has great influence with me."

Ironically, Lucy Hayes is best known for something she was not responsible for—refusing to serve alcohol in the White House. At the first diplomatic dinner of the new administration, in honor of visitors from Russia, many kinds of wine were served. When newspapers reported on the dinner, temperance groups complained bitterly. They had hoped that the Hayes White House would set a good example by refusing to serve alcohol.

The temperance movement had a huge following at the time, and most who supported it also voted for Republicans. After the outcry about the dinner for the Russians, Rutherford and Lucy decided together that they would not serve alcohol at future White House functions. They knew the decision would cause unhappiness to some and would bring ridicule from others. Yet they believed it was a wise decision to keep supporters of temperance from forming their own political party.

Some critics of the policy blamed it on Lucy's beliefs. While she did not drink alcohol herself, she had never tried to keep others from it. Behind her back, some may have called her "Lemonade Lucy," but the name did not appear in print until many years later.

Lucy also began the annual Easter Egg Roll for children on the White House Lawn in 1878, a tradition that continues today.

★★☆

Lucy Hayes (center), surrounded by a group of young women who helped plan White House social events.

The States During the Presidency of Rutherford B. Hayes

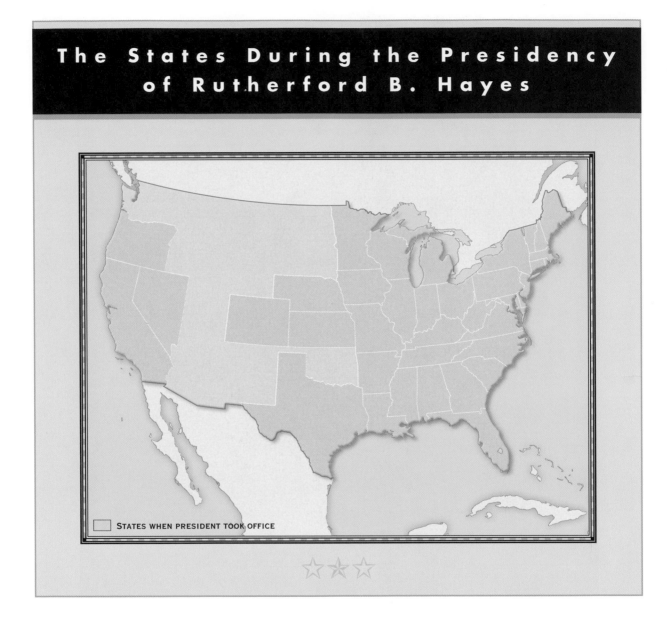

STATES WHEN PRESIDENT TOOK OFFICE

⭐ ⭐ ☆

New Technology in the White House

During Hayes's presidency, new inventions were changing the way people worked and communicated. The telegraph already allowed people to send messages across the country almost instantly. In 1877, 30-year-old Alexander Graham Bell was demonstrating his telephone, which could carry the sound of a human voice by wire. In June, Bell spoke to President Hayes in the White House over 13 miles (21 km) of wire. Soon afterward, Hayes had a telephone installed in the White House.

The following year, young Thomas Edison brought his phonograph to the White House, demonstrating one of the first devices that could record and play back sounds, including voices or music. Hayes also brought the first typewriter into the White House and had the first permanent running water system installed there. An enthusiastic believer in new technology, Hayes saw it as a way to improve the lives of all Americans.

☆ ☆ ☆

was tried, with the Senate serving as the jury, and missed being convicted by only one vote. During Grant's presidency, Congress continued to make many of the decisions. Although Grant was personally popular, he usually followed the recommendations of Republican leaders in Congress.

Hayes brought an independent spirit to the White House. He made controversial appointments to his cabinet, and managed to get all of them approved by the Senate. In the case of the New York Custom House, he faced down powerful Republicans in the Senate and gained a major victory.

Congress continued to test him. In important bills appropriating money to keep government running, Congressional leaders buried *riders* (clauses unrelated to the purpose of the bill). One such rider would have taken away protections for African Americans' rights in the South. Hayes angrily vetoed these bills and requested Congress to submit bills without such riders. In the end, they were forced to do as he requested. Congress continued to wield considerable power, but Hayes helped restore the balance between president and Congress. This proved to be an important legacy for later presidents.

Chapter 5

A New President ──────────────

In his inaugural address, Rutherford Hayes had promised to serve only one term as president. He believed that he could be a better president if he did not have to worry about being reelected. Early in 1880, he made it clear to the party that he would not be a candidate in that year's presidential election.

Soon there was a rush of Republican candidates hoping to win the nomination. At the Republican convention that summer, former president Grant, who had spent much of the past four years traveling, was placed in nomination for a third term. He was supported by Senator Conkling of New York and the party faction that called themselves the Stalwarts. James G. Blaine, who had lost the nomination to Hayes in 1876, was also placed in nomination. Finally, Hayes's secretary of the treasury, John Sherman of Ohio, was nominated by James

Garfield, a congressional leader from Ohio, in a dramatic speech that electrified the huge crowd of delegates.

After 34 long roll-call votes, no one of the three candidates could gain the required votes to win the nomination. Delegates were exhausted and began looking for a new candidate who could win. Finally, supporters of Blaine and Sherman agreed that they could all vote for James Garfield, whose speech had so inspired the convention. Garfield won the Republican nomination on the 36th ballot. In order to gain support from the Stalwart faction, the convention nominated Chester A. Arthur of New York for vice president. President Hayes, who had removed Arthur from his post at the New York Custom House, was surprised.

In November, Garfield was elected in a contest nearly as close as the election of 1876. Out of more than 9 million votes cast, Garfield won only 10,000 more than Democratic candidate Winfield Scott Hancock. Fortunately, he won a clear majority in the electoral college, and gained election without dispute.

Hayes was pleased to turn over the reins of the government to an old friend and associate, a Republican and an Ohioan. Near the end of his term in March 1881, he wrote, "Nobody ever left the Presidency with less regret, less disappointment, fewer heart burnings, or more general content . . . than I do."

A Republican poster for James Garfield and Chester Arthur in the 1880 presidential campaign.

A magazine cartoon in March 1881 shows Liberty offering a laurel wreath to Rutherford Hayes, who has retired from the presidency, and greeting James Garfield, who has just taken office.

Even though Hayes and Garfield were both Ohioans and rose to general-ships during the Civil War, they had rarely crossed paths. They served together briefly in the House of Representatives in the 1860s. After that, Hayes had returned to Ohio. Garfield had remained in Washington, becoming a Republican leader in the House. Early in 1880, he had been elected to the U.S. Senate, but he resigned before serving a single day to become president.

Garfield began his presidency as Hayes had begun his—with a fight against Senator Roscoe Conkling over appointments to federal offices. When Garfield won, Conkling resigned his Senate seat in protest. But then, on July 2, 1881, in a Washington train station, Garfield was shot by an assassin. The assassin, Charles Guiteau, was captured immediately after the shooting. "I am a Stalwart," he said, "and now Arthur [also a Stalwart] is president." The nation was shocked. It soon turned out that Guiteau was a disturbed person who carried out the assassination by himself. Arthur and the Stalwarts knew nothing of his actions.

For months, Garfield hovered between life and death. Then on September 19, he died. Chester Arthur was sworn in as president. Arthur surprised many who feared that he would end the movement toward civil service reform. In fact, he supported and signed the Pendleton Civil Service Act, which had its beginning in the Hayes administration.

When James Garfield died in September 1881, Chester A. Arthur (above) became president.

A Busy Ex-President

The Hayes family returned to their elegant home at Spiegel Grove, in Fremont, Ohio. "We wish to get as completely back into private life as we can," Hayes told a friend. Hayes refused to get involved in national politics, but he pursued an active life of public service. He raised money for the local town library, became director of a new savings bank, and was named a trustee of his wife's Methodist church, although he did not become a member himself. He was elected "noble grand" of the local chapter of the Odd Fellows, a fraternal organization, and was an enthusiastic participant in reunions of the Grand Army of the Republic (GAR), a national organization of Union veterans of the Civil War.

A Friend of Education

The cause that Hayes was most committed to in retirement was education. He became a trustee of Ohio State University, the institution he had helped found as governor, and served on the boards of several other colleges. Convinced that education would help the South rise from the ruins of the Civil War, Hayes raised nearly $3,500,000 for education in that region. In 1882 he became president of the Slater Fund, which gave hundreds of African Americans an opportunity to get a secondary or college education. Among those helped was W. E. B. Du Bois,

Above, the handsome house at Spiegel Grove, where Rutherford and Lucy Hayes lived in retirement. At right, the Hayes family gathers around the retired president. From left to right: son Birchard Hayes, his wife Mary, the president, son Scott Hayes, son Rutherford P. Hayes, Lucy, daughter Fanny Hayes, and son James Webb Hayes.

who was later a founder of the National Association for the Advancement of Colored People (NAACP).

Hayes also became active in prison reform. From 1883 to his death he was president of the National Prison Association. He urged prison officials to provide

Prison Reform in America

Punishment for serious crime in early America was swift. Depending on the crime, a convicted criminal could be branded on the thumb, whipped, or put to death. Imprisonment was not an option. Criminals sat in jail only to await trial or punishment.

This changed in the late 1700s, when large prisons began to appear. The first was Philadelphia's Walnut Street Jail, opened in 1790. Long jail sentences and solitary confinement became regular punishments. Early prisons were called penitentiaries because one goal was to make prisoners penitent, or sorry, for their crimes.

Reformers, including Hayes, sought ways to rehabilitate prisoners through education and work training. The Elmira Reformatory in New York was a model prison when it opened in 1876. Prisoners were rewarded for good behavior and some received *parole*, or early release. Inmates with education organized elementary classes for other inmates at night.

Prison reform remains a subject of debate to the present day. Reformers have learned that it may not be possible to rehabilitate all criminals, but they continue to fight for better conditions for prisoners in hopes of ending the cycle of crime in America.

☆ ☆ ☆

education and job training as a way to reform convicted criminals and return them to society as responsible, law-abiding citizens.

The Last Chapter

In June 1889, Lucy Hayes suffered a serious stroke. Three days later, she died at the age of 57. Her husband was devastated by her death, but looked to the promises of religion for comfort. "She is in Heaven," he said. "She is where all the best of earth have gone."

To forget his grief, Hayes buried himself in work. "Busy as ever— busier!" he wrote at age 69 to a friend. "Shoeing [hiking] on to the end!"

In January 1893, Hayes visited his wife's grave in a horse-drawn sleigh. The next day he traveled to Columbus by train to attend a meeting of the Ohio State University board of trustees. While there, he met with his old friend, Ohio governor William McKinley, who had served as a young officer under Hayes's command in the Civil War. (McKinley would be elected president in 1896.)

After continuing on to Cleveland for more business, Hayes was waiting for a train home with his son Webb when he suddenly experienced chest pains. Webb urged his father to put off the trip and seek treatment, but Hayes refused. "I would rather die at Spiegel Grove than to live anywhere else," he said.

The memorial stone at the gravesite of Rutherford Hayes at Spiegel Grove in Fremont, Ohio.

Hayes got his wish, dying on January 17, 1893, in his own bed of heart failure. His last recorded words were, "I know that I am going where Lucy is."

Among those attending Hayes's funeral were Republican president Benjamin Harrison and president-elect Grover Cleveland. Harrison was just completing his term, and Cleveland was about to take office for the second time. He had already served as president from 1885 to 1889. The presence of both Republican and Democratic presidents was a sign that the disputed election of 1876 had been forgotten. Hayes's record as president had long ago overcome the talk of a stolen election. He had proved by his words and actions that he was no fraud. He was the real thing, a worthy president of the United States.

Hayes was buried in Oakwood Cemetery in Fremont. Years later, his remains were moved to the family burial plot at Spiegel Grove, where Lucy and other family members are also buried. The house and grounds at Spiegel Grove are now part of the Rutherford B. Hayes Presidential Center.

Chapter 6

A Good President

In the gallery of American presidents, Rutherford B. Hayes is ranked by historians as above average, a well-intentioned president who tried to do good and often succeeded.

"He was not a great president but he was a good one," wrote T. Harry Williams. "Solid and capable, he grew in his office and left that office stronger than he found it."

A Gentleman in Politics

Many earlier presidents had based their political lives on the hope of becoming president. By contrast, Hayes had been satisfied to pursue a successful political career in Ohio. He ran for president as an outsider, untouched by the scandals in Washington. He was honored and pleased to be elected president, but he often found the demands of the office both difficult and tiresome.

Rutherford B. Hayes

He came to office in a time of great change. The grave disputes and trials of the Civil War were fading in people's memory, and attention was turning to a new set of problems. Hayes dealt with the still divisive issues of Reconstruction in the South, but he was also able to look forward. He was a pioneer in pressing for reform of federal appointments, and his battles to end corrupt practices helped lead to the Pendleton Civil Service Act, signed in 1883, and later civil service reforms.

Ohio, Cradle of Presidents

Hayes was the second of seven presidents born in Ohio, after Ulysses S. Grant. Between 1881 and 1921, five more Ohio natives would take up the office. All seven Ohio presidents were Republicans. Ohio is the birthplace of more presidents than any state except Virginia, which claims eight. The Ohio presidents are:

President	Birthplace and year	Years in presidency
Ulysses S. Grant	Point Pleasant, 1822	1869–1877
Rutherford B. Hayes	Delaware, 1822	1877–1881
James A. Garfield	Orange Township, 1831	1881
Benjamin Harrison	North Bend, 1833	1889–1893
William McKinley	Niles, 1843	1897–1901
William Howard Taft	Cincinnati, 1857	1909–1913
Warren G. Harding	Blooming Grove, 1865	1921–1923

☆☆☆

Only three presidents are known to have kept diaries during their presidency: John Quincy Adams, James K. Polk, and Rutherford B. Hayes. Hayes's diary is notable for its chatty, good-natured mood, and its amusing descriptions of ordinary life. According to T. Harry Williams, who edited a published version, the diary is "one of the best accounts penned of the social and routine life of a president."

The diary reveals that Hayes always had a sense of humor even about himself. He was not taken in by the praise and flattery he so often heard as president and was aware of his own strengths and weaknesses.

A page from Hayes's diary.

On the last day of his presidency, Hayes wrote, "Never have I listened to as much commendation as I heard yesterday. Mrs. Hayes seems to be a great and almost universal favorite. Would we were worthier."

☆ ★ ☆

Hayes also recognized the dangers of big business. Political leaders were being wooed and pressured by railroads and other large corporations for special treatment and government favors. He warned against "government of the corporations, by the corporations and for the corporations." Both in his own behavior and in his appointments, he sought to keep the government at arm's length from entanglement with business.

Hayes brought a strong sense of morality to the White House at a time when many politicians seemed most interested in increasing their own power and wealth. He was known as a "gentleman in politics" and was a model public servant. Even though the circumstances that brought him to the White House were suspect, Hayes left the presidency widely admired and praised for his performance, bringing honor to his country, his party, and himself.

Compromise or Betrayal? —————————————

The one act of Hayes's presidency that runs against his reputation was the decision to end Reconstruction. When the last troops left the South, Hayes hoped fervently that white leaders there would agree to grant basic rights to their former slaves. Instead, they passed ever more restrictive laws, forbidding African Americans to live among whites, go to school with whites, sit with whites in public places, or even use the same restrooms.

Withdrawing troops from the remaining southern states may have been part of the "compromise" that brought Hayes to the White House. In any case, it was a popular action, and one that Hayes approved. Citizens were exhausted by the long battle to protect the rights of African Americans. It seemed that continuing to use military forces would never solve the problem.

Still, students of civil rights do not consider the end of Reconstruction a mild compromise. They consider it a betrayal of promises made at the end of the Civil War.

The Judgment of History

Rutherford B. Hayes was not an inspiring speaker or an architect of great new ideas. He was a straightforward man with a modest view of himself. During the Civil War he proved to be a leader who could inspire and gain his troops' undying loyalty. His judgment of others, including those he appointed to high positions, was shrewd and accurate. Even though he won the presidency in a controversial election, there were no major scandals in his presidency. Not the greatest or most successful of presidents, he had done much better than most.

Perhaps the best tribute to Hayes was written after he left office by his secretary of the treasury, John Sherman, who wrote, "Among the multitude of public men I have met, I have known no one who held a higher sense of his duty to his country, and more faithfully discharged that duty, than President Hayes."

Fast Facts Rutherford B. Hayes

Birth:	October 4, 1822
Birthplace:	Delaware, Ohio
Parents:	Rutherford Hayes Jr. and Sophia Birchard Hayes
Brothers & Sisters:	Lorenzo (1815–1825); Fanny Arabella (1820–1856)
Education:	Kenyon College, Gambier, Ohio, graduated 1842
	Harvard Law School, Cambridge, Massachusetts, graduated 1845
Occupation:	Lawyer
Marriage:	To Lucy Ware Webb, December 30, 1852
Children:	(*See* First Lady Fast Facts at right)
Political Party:	Republican
Government Service:	1858–1861 City Solicitor, Cincinnati, Ohio
	1861–1865 Officer, Union Army
	1865–1867 U.S. House of Representatives
	1868–1872 Governor of Ohio
	1876 Governor of Ohio
	1877–1881 19th President of the United States
His Vice President:	William Almon Wheeler
Major Actions as President:	1877 Removed federal troops from South Carolina and Louisiana, ending Reconstruction
	1877 Sent federal troops to end violence in the Great Railroad Strike
	1878 Suspended the head of the New York Custom House after reports of corruption
	1880 Visited California and Oregon
Firsts:	First president to put a telephone in the White House
	First president to visit Pacific Coast during his presidency
Death:	January 17, 1893
Age at Death:	70 years
Burial Place:	Oakwood Cemetery, Fremont, Ohio
	(Later moved to Spiegel Grove in Fremont)

Fast Facts Lucy Ware Webb Hayes

Birth:	August 28, 1831
Birthplace:	Chillicothe, Ohio
Parents:	Dr. James and Maria Cook Webb
Brothers & Sisters:	Joseph Thomson (1827–1880)
	James Dewees (1828–1873)
Education:	Wesleyan College, Delaware, Ohio
	Wesleyan Female College, Cincinnati, Ohio, graduated 1850
Marriage:	To Rutherford B. Hayes, December 30, 1852
Children:	Birchard Austin (1853–1926)
	James Webb Cook (1856–1934)
	Rutherford Platt (1858–1927)
	Joseph Thompson (1861–1863)
	George Crook (1864–1866)
	Fanny (1867–1950)
	Scott Russell (1871–1923)
	Mannin Force (1873–1874)
Firsts:	First wife of a president to earn a college degree
	Established Easter Egg Roll for children on the White House Lawn in 1878
Death:	June 25, 1889 in Fremont, Ohio
Age at Death:	58 years
Burial Place:	Oakwood Cemetery, Fremont, Ohio
	(later moved to Spiegel Grove in Fremont)

Timeline

1822	1838	1842	1843	1845
Rutherford Birchard Hayes born October 4.	Enters Kenyon College in Gambier, Ohio.	Graduates from Kenyon first in his class.	Enrolls at Harvard Law School, graduates 1845.	Licensed to practice law: begins practice in Lower Sandusky (later Fremont), Ohio.

1861	1862	1864	1865	1866
The Civil War begins, April 12; Hayes enlists.	Wounded at the Battle of South Mountain in Maryland on September 14.	Wounded at Cedar Creek, Virginia; elected to the U.S. Congress.	Confederate States surrender; Hayes resigns from the army, June 8.	Wins second term in the House of Representatives.

1877	1877	1877	1880	1881
Electoral Commission declares Hayes president, March 2; Hayes sworn in March 3 and again in public ceremony March 5.	Orders the last federal troops out of the South, ending Reconstruction, April.	Sends in federal troops to end the Great Railroad Strike, July.	Becomes the first president to visit the West Coast, touring California and Oregon.	James A. Garfield takes office as 20th president; Hayes returns to Fremont, Ohio.

1850	1852	1858	1859	1860
Opens law office in Cincinnati, Ohio.	Marries Lucy Ware Webb, December 30.	Appointed city solicitor of Cincinnati.	Wins election as city solicitor.	Abraham Lincoln elected president.

1867	1868	1872	1875	1876
Resigns from Congress; elected governor of Ohio, serves 1868–1872.	President Andrew Johnson impeached by the House, but acquitted by the Senate.	Hayes defeated for Congress and retires to Fremont, Ohio.	Elected to a third term as governor of Ohio.	Receives Republican nomination for president, June; election results contested, November.

1881	1889	1893
Garfield is shot, July; dies of his wounds, September; Chester A. Arthur becomes 21st president.	Lucy Hayes dies, June 25.	Hayes dies January 17 at Spiegel Grove, his Ohio home.

Glossary

abolitionist: in the mid-1800s, a person who believed that slavery was a moral wrong and should be ended (or abolished) immediately

ballot: a vote, especially one to choose nominees at a political convention; if no one wins the required number, additional ballots are taken until there is a winner

brevet: a temporary promotion in military rank, often given as a recognition of bravery; Hayes became a brevet major general in 1864

Free-Soiler: in the mid-1800s, a member of the Free-Soil party, which opposed the spread of slavery to new U.S. territories

impeach: in U.S. government, to formally accuse a high official of a serious crime; the impeached official stands trial on the charges and is removed from office if convicted

override: in U.S. government, the action of a legislature to make a bill a law after the executive has vetoed it; the U.S. Congress may override a president's veto by passing the bill by two-thirds majorities in the House and the Senate

parole: in the justice system, release of a prisoner before his or her sentence has been served, based on good behavior

rider: a clause in a legislative bill designed to accomplish something unrelated to the bill's main purpose

secede: to withdraw from a government; southern states seceded from the United States in 1861

segregation: separation of people, especially by race; after the end of Reconstruction, southern governments passed laws segregating African Americans from white citizens

solicitor: a lawyer who represents a government; Hayes was city solicitor of Cincinnati

Union: in the mid-1800s, a common word for the United States; in the Civil War, the northern side was known as the Union

veto: in U.S. government, the refusal of a chief executive (such as the president) to sign a bill passed by the legislature (such as Congress) into law

Further Reading

Anthony, Carl Sferrazza. *America's First Families: An Inside View of 200 Years of Private Life in the White House.* New York: Touchstone, 2000.

Blassingame, Wyatt. *The Look-It-Up Book of Presidents.* Revised edition. New York: Random House, 1996.

Cooke, Donald E. *Presidents in Uniform.* New York: Hastings House, 1969.

Diller, Daniel C., and Stephen L. Robertson. *The Presidents, First Ladies, and Vice Presidents: White House Biographies, 1789–2001.* Washington, DC: CQ Press, 2001.

Weymouth, Lally. *America in 1876: The Way We Were.* New York: Random House, 1976.

Whitney, David C., and Robin Vaughn Whitney. *The American Presidents.* 8th edition. Pleasantville, NY: Reader's Digest Association, 1996.

MORE ADVANCED READING

Barnard, Harry. *Rutherford B. Hayes and His America.* Indianapolis: Bobbs-Merrill, 1954.

Hoogenboom, Ari. *Rutherford B. Hayes: Warrior and President*. Lawrence: University Press of Kansas, 1995.

Williams, T. Harry, editor. *Hayes: The Diary of a President 1875–1881.* New York: David McKay, 1964.

Places to Visit

The Rutherford B. Hayes Presidential
Center
Spiegel Grove
Fremont, OH 43420
(800) 998-7737
A museum and library established on the
estate where Rutherford and Lucy Hayes
lived in retirement. Also contains the
burial site of Rutherford and Lucy. The
bookstore offers a prize-winning CD-ROM
on Hayes and his presidency. Visit the
center's Web site (*see* next page) for
further information.

Cincinnati History Museum
Cincinnati Museum Center
1301 Western Avenue
Cincinnati, OH 45203-1130
(513) 287-7000 or (800) 733-2077
Museum exhibits include portrayals of life
in Cincinnati in the 1850s, when Hayes
lived there and practiced law.

Carnifex Ferry Battlefield State Park
Route 2, Box 435
Summersville, WV 26651
(304) 872-0825 or (800) CALL WVA
The site of the first battle where Hayes and
the 23rd Ohio saw action in late 1861.

Cedar Creek Battlefield Visitors Center
Cedar Creek and Belle Grove National
Historical Park
Office: 7718 1/2 Main Street
Middletown, VA 22645
Mail: P.O. Box 229
Strasburg, VA 22657
The site of the last battle Hayes fought in.
He was promoted to brevet major general
for his contribution to a Union victory.

Ohio Statehouse Education and
Visitors Center
The Ohio State House
Broad and High Streets
Columbus, OH 43215
(614) 728-2695 or (614) 752-6350 *(tour*
information recording*)* (888) OHIO-123
(toll-free tour information recording)
Hayes served two terms as governor here
in Columbus.

The White House
1600 Pennsylvania Avenue NW
Washington, DC 20500
Visitors' Office (202) 456-7041
The Hayes's home from 1877 to 1881. For
more information, visit the White House
Web site (*see* next page).

Online Sites of Interest

★ **Internet Public Library: Presidents of the United States (IPL POTUS)**

http://www.ipl.org/div/potus/rbhayes.html

Includes concise information about Hayes and his presidency, and useful links to other Internet sites.

★ **AmericanPresident.org**

http://www.americanpresident.org/history/rutherfordhayes

An opening thumbnail biography is supported by pages with more detailed information on Hayes's early life, political career, and presidency. The site is operated by the Miller Center of Public Affairs at the University of Virginia.

★ **Rutherford B. Hayes Presidential Center**

http://www.rbhayes.org

Contains extensive information on Hayes and his family, including recent scholarly articles about his presidency. Also includes information on Ohio history during Hayes's lifetime.

★ **Hayes's Inaugural Address**

http://memory.loc.gov/ammem/pihtml/pi026.html

Hayes's complete inaugural address is here as well as photographs of his inauguration and other archival material. The inaugural address of every president can be accessed on this site.

★ **The White House**

http://www.whitehouse.gov

Information about the current president and vice president; White House history and tours; biographies of past presidents and their families; a virtual tour of the historic building; current events; trivia quizzes; and much more. Also includes a site with information of special interest to kids.

Table of Presidents

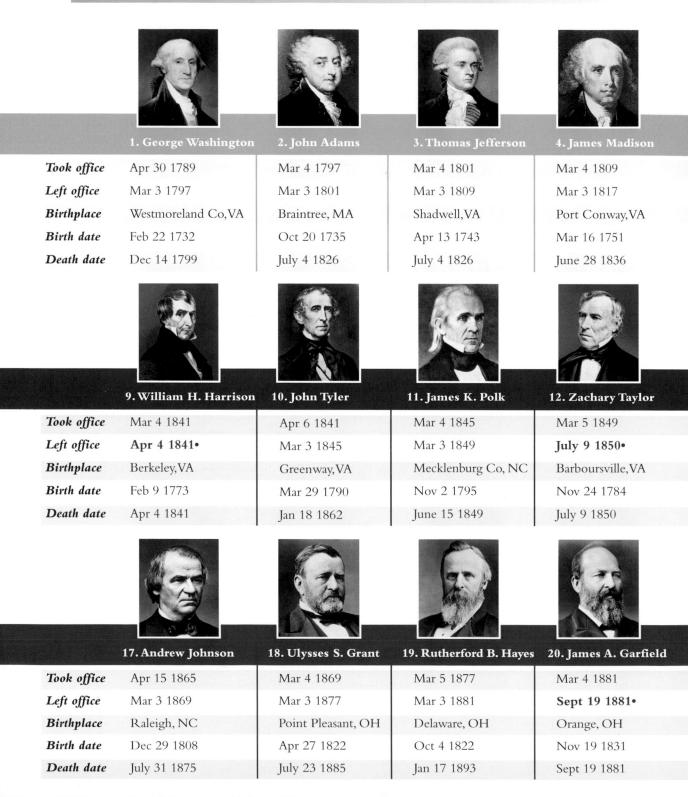

	1. George Washington	**2. John Adams**	**3. Thomas Jefferson**	**4. James Madison**
Took office	Apr 30 1789	Mar 4 1797	Mar 4 1801	Mar 4 1809
Left office	Mar 3 1797	Mar 3 1801	Mar 3 1809	Mar 3 1817
Birthplace	Westmoreland Co, VA	Braintree, MA	Shadwell, VA	Port Conway, VA
Birth date	Feb 22 1732	Oct 20 1735	Apr 13 1743	Mar 16 1751
Death date	Dec 14 1799	July 4 1826	July 4 1826	June 28 1836

	9. William H. Harrison	**10. John Tyler**	**11. James K. Polk**	**12. Zachary Taylor**
Took office	Mar 4 1841	Apr 6 1841	Mar 4 1845	Mar 5 1849
Left office	**Apr 4 1841•**	Mar 3 1845	Mar 3 1849	**July 9 1850•**
Birthplace	Berkeley, VA	Greenway, VA	Mecklenburg Co, NC	Barboursville, VA
Birth date	Feb 9 1773	Mar 29 1790	Nov 2 1795	Nov 24 1784
Death date	Apr 4 1841	Jan 18 1862	June 15 1849	July 9 1850

	17. Andrew Johnson	**18. Ulysses S. Grant**	**19. Rutherford B. Hayes**	**20. James A. Garfield**
Took office	Apr 15 1865	Mar 4 1869	Mar 5 1877	Mar 4 1881
Left office	Mar 3 1869	Mar 3 1877	Mar 3 1881	**Sept 19 1881•**
Birthplace	Raleigh, NC	Point Pleasant, OH	Delaware, OH	Orange, OH
Birth date	Dec 29 1808	Apr 27 1822	Oct 4 1822	Nov 19 1831
Death date	July 31 1875	July 23 1885	Jan 17 1893	Sept 19 1881

5. James Monroe

Mar 4 1817

Mar 3 1825

Westmoreland Co, VA

Apr 28 1758

July 4 1831

6. John Quincy Adams

Mar 4 1825

Mar 3 1829

Braintree, MA

July 11 1767

Feb 23 1848

7. Andrew Jackson

Mar 4 1829

Mar 3 1837

The Waxhaws, SC

Mar 15 1767

June 8 1845

8. Martin Van Buren

Mar 4 1837

Mar 3 1841

Kinderhook, NY

Dec 5 1782

July 24 1862

13. Millard Fillmore

July 9 1850

Mar 3 1853

Locke Township, NY

Jan 7 1800

Mar 8 1874

14. Franklin Pierce

Mar 4 1853

Mar 3 1857

Hillsborough, NH

Nov 23 1804

Oct 8 1869

15. James Buchanan

Mar 4 1857

Mar 3 1861

Cove Gap, PA

Apr 23 1791

June 1 1868

16. Abraham Lincoln

Mar 4 1861

Apr 15 1865•

Hardin Co, KY

Feb 12 1809

Apr 15 1865

21. Chester A. Arthur

Sept 19 1881

Mar 3 1885

Fairfield, VT

Oct 5 1829

Nov 18 1886

22. Grover Cleveland

Mar 4 1885

Mar 3 1889

Caldwell, NJ

Mar 18 1837

June 24 1908

23. Benjamin Harrison

Mar 4 1889

Mar 3 1893

North Bend, OH

Aug 20 1833

Mar 13 1901

24. Grover Cleveland

Mar 4 1893

Mar 3 1897

Caldwell, NJ

Mar 18 1837

June 24 1908

	25. William McKinley	26. Theodore Roosevelt	27. William H. Taft	28. Woodrow Wilson
Took office	Mar 4 1897	Sept 14 1901	Mar 4 1909	Mar 4 1913
Left office	**Sept 14 1901•**	Mar 3 1909	Mar 3 1913	Mar 3 1921
Birthplace	Niles, OH	New York, NY	Cincinnati, OH	Staunton, VA
Birth date	Jan 29 1843	Oct 27 1858	Sept 15 1857	Dec 28 1856
Death date	Sept 14 1901	Jan 6 1919	Mar 8 1930	Feb 3 1924

	33. Harry S. Truman	34. Dwight D. Eisenhower	35. John F. Kennedy	36. Lyndon B. Johnson
Took office	Apr 12 1945	Jan 20 1953	Jan 20 1961	Nov 22 1963
Left office	Jan 20 1953	Jan 20 1961	**Nov 22 1963•**	Jan 20 1969
Birthplace	Lamar, MO	Denison, TX	Brookline, MA	Johnson City, TX
Birth date	May 8 1884	Oct 14 1890	May 29 1917	Aug 27 1908
Death date	Dec 26 1972	Mar 28 1969	Nov 22 1963	Jan 22 1973

	41. George Bush	42. Bill Clinton	43. George W. Bush	
Took office	Jan 20 1989	Jan 20 1993	Jan 20 2001	
Left office	Jan 20 1993	Jan 20 2001	—	
Birthplace	Milton, MA	Hope, AR	New Haven, CT	
Birth date	June 12 1924	Aug 19 1946	July 6 1946	
Death date	—	—	—	

29. Warren G. Harding	30. Calvin Coolidge	31. Herbert Hoover	32. Franklin D. Roosevelt
Mar 4 1921	Aug 2 1923	Mar 4 1929	Mar 4 1933
Aug 2 1923•	Mar 3 1929	Mar 3 1933	**Apr 12 1945•**
Blooming Grove, OH	Plymouth, VT	West Branch, IA	Hyde Park, NY
Nov 21 1865	July 4 1872	Aug 10 1874	Jan 30 1882
Aug 2 1923	Jan 5 1933	Oct 20 1964	Apr 12 1945

37. Richard M. Nixon	38. Gerald R. Ford	39. Jimmy Carter	40. Ronald Reagan
Jan 20 1969	Aug 9 1974	Jan 20 1977	Jan 20 1981
Aug 9 1974★	Jan 20 1977	Jan 20 1981	Jan 20 1989
Yorba Linda, CA	Omaha, NE	Plains, GA	Tampico, IL
Jan 9 1913	July 14 1913	Oct 1 1924	Feb 11 1911
Apr 22 1994	—	—	—

• Indicates the president died while in office.

★ Richard Nixon resigned before his term expired.

Index

Page numbers in *italics* indicate illustrations.

abolitionists, 21
African Americans, 33, 35–36, 57–58, 74, 81,
    93–94
alcohol/temperance movement, 70
Appomattox Court House, Virginia, 29
Arthur, Chester A., 60, 61, *61,* 79

Bell, Alexander Graham, 73
Birchard, Sardis (uncle of Rutherford B.
    Hayes), 12, 13–14, 15, 38
Blaine, James G., 42, 75
Bland-Allison bill, 62
Bradley, Joseph, 51
Bristow, Benjamin, 42
Buckland, Ralph, 14
Bush, George W., 7

Centennial Exhibition, *44,* 44–45, *45*
Cheat Mountain Pass, 26
Chinese immigrants, 66, 68
Cincinnati, Ohio, 14–15, *16*
civil rights, 35–36, 74, 93–94
civil service system, 47
Civil War, 24, *25,* 27
    fast facts, 27
Cleveland, Grover, 28, 87
Colfax, Schuyler, 40
Collector of the Port of New York, 60
Columbus, Ohio, *37*
Congress, 69, 73–74
Conkling, Roscoe, 42, 75, 79
Corbin, Abel, 40
Corliss engine, 44, *45*
corruption, 40, 42, 58, 60, 61
Crédit Mobilier scandal, 40
Custom House, 60

Davis, David, 48, 51

Democratic convention (1876), 46–47
depression, economic, 62
diaries, 92
discrimination, 57–58, 93–94
Du Bois, W.E.B., 81–84

Early, Jubal, 27
Easter Egg Roll, 70
economy, 62
Edison, Thomas, 73
education, 81
election of 1876, 7–9, 47–48, 51
election of 1880, 76
election of 2000, 7
Electoral Commission, 8, 48, 51, *52*
Evarts, William M., 58

Farrer, Nancy, 15, 17
Fisk, Jim, 40
Free-Soilers, 21
Frémont, John Charles, 14–15, 22
Fremont, Ohio, 14–15

Garfield, James A., 28, 55, 75–76, *78, 79,
    80*
Gore, Albert, 7
Gould, Jay, 40
government
    Bland-Allison bill, 62
    civil service system, 47, 61
    Congress, 69, 73–74
    Electoral Commission, 8, 48, 51, *52*
    Fifteenth Amendment to Constitution,
        35–36
    Kansas-Nebraska Act, 22
    Pendleton Civil Service Act, 61
    riders on Congressional bills, 74
    spoils system, 58, 60, 61
    U.S. Congress, *49*
Granger, Daniel, 11

Grant, Ulysses S., 28, *30,* 35, 38, 39, 40, 42, *56,* 73, 75

Great Railroad Strike, 63, *64, 65,* 66

Guiteau, Charles, 79

Hall of Machinery, 44, *44*

Hancock, Winfield Scott, 76

Harrison, Benjamin, 28, 87

Harvard Law School, 13

Hayes, Birchard (son of Rutherford B.), 19, *83*

Hayes, Fanny (daughter of Rutherford B.), *83*

Hayes, James Webb Cook (son of Rutherford B.), 24, *83*

Hayes, Joseph Thompson (son of Rutherford B.), 26, 27

Hayes, Lorenzo (brother of Rutherford B.), 9, 10

Hayes, Lucy Ware Webb (wife of Rutherford B.), *18, 71, 83*

    children, 19, 24, 26, 27, 69

    courtship, 17

    death, 85

    education, 17

    family values, 69

    fast facts, 97

    first lady, 70

    marriage, 19

    military wife, 26–27

Hayes, Mary (daughter-in-law of Rutherford B.), *83*

Hayes, Rutherford, Jr. (father of Rutherford B.), 9

Hayes, Rutherford Birchard, *18, 23, 34, 78, 83, 90*

    birth/birthplace, 9, *10*

    cabinet appointments, 58, 60

    campaign for nomination (1876), 42, 46–47

    childhood, 10–12

    children, 19, 24, 26, 27, 69

    city solicitor, 24

    conflicts with congress, 69, 73–74

    congressman, 29, 31, 33, 35

Hayes, Rutherford Birchard (cont'd.)

    courtship, 17

    death, 87

    diary, 92, *92*

    education, 11, 12–13

    election of 1876, 7–9, 47–48, 51

    family home, 38, *82*

    family portrait, *83*

    family values, 69

    fast facts, 96

    foreign affairs, 68

    governor, 35–36, 38, 42

    inauguration, 54, 55, *56,* 75

    lawyer, 14–15, 17, 21

    lecturer, 17

    legacy, 89, 91, 93–95

    marriage, 19

    military career, 24, 26–29, 31

    presidency, 58, 60, 62–63, 66, 68–69, 73–76

    reforms, prisons and mental hospitals, 36, 84–85

    retirement, 38, 76, 81, 84–85

    states during presidency, map of, *72*

    timeline, 98–99

    travel to Western states, 66, *67,* 68

Hayes, Rutherford Platt (son of Rutherford B.), *83*

Hayes, Sara (sister of Rutherford B.), 9

Hayes, Scott Russell (son of Rutherford B.), *83*

Hayes, Sophia Birchard (mother of Rutherford B.), 9

Herron, John W., 15

Isaac Webb's Preparatory School, 12

Johnson, Andrew, 33, 35, 69, 73

Kansas-Nebraska Act, 22

Kenyon College, 12

Key, David, 58

Lee, Robert E., 29, *30*

Liberal Republicans, 59
Lincoln, Abraham, 24
Lower Sandusky, Ohio, 14

Machinery Hall, 44, *44*
manufacturing, 36
McKinley, William, 28, 85
memorial stone, *86*
military occupation, southern states, 51, 57
mining, 36

National Association for the Advancement of
        Colored People (NAACP), 84
Native Americans, 66
New York Custom House, 50
Norwalk Academy, 12

Ohio Agricultural and Mechanical College, 36
Ohio River, *16*
Ohio State University, 36, 81

Pendleton Civil Service Act, 61
phonograph, 73
Platt, Emily (niece of Rutherford B. Hayes), 69
Platt, Fanny Hayes (sister of Rutherford B.
        Hayes), 9, 10–11, 22
political cartoons
    election of 1876, *8*
    Hayes and Garfield, *78*
    Jay Gould scandals, *41*
    scandals during Grant presidency, *43*
political parties, 22, 33, 42, 59, 75, 79
presidential campaign poster (1880), *77*
presidents
    born in Ohio, 91
    served in the Civil War, 28
prison reform, 84–85

racism, 57–58, 93–94
Radical Republicans, 33, 35
railroads, 63, *64, 65,* 66
Reconstruction, 33, 57, 93–94

Republican convention (1875), 46
Republican party, 22, 42
Rutherford B. Hayes Presidential Center, 15, 87

scandals, 40, 42
Schurz, Carl, 58, 59, *59*
segregation, 57–58, 93–94
Sheridan, Philip, 29
Sherman, John, 58, 75, 94–95
shipping, 14
slavery, 21
Spiegel Grove (Hayes family home), 38, *82*
spoils system, 58, 60, 61
Stalwarts, 42, 75, 79
State House (Ohio), 37
states during Hayes's presidency, map of, *72*
Story, Joseph, 13

taxes, 60
technology, 73
telegraph, 73
telephone, 73
temperance movement, 70
Tilden, Samuel J., 7–8, 46–47, 47, 50, *50*
trade, 14
Tweed, William "Boss," 50
Tweed Ring, 51

Union Depot, Pittsburgh, *64*
U.S. Congress, *49*

voting rights, 36

War of 1812, 9
Webb, Joseph (brother-in-law of Rutherford
        B. Hayes), 26
Wheeler, William Almon, 46, 68
"Whiskey Ring," 40
Williams, T. Harry, 89, 92
Wilson, Henry, 40

Yosemite Valley, *67*

About the Author

Steven Otfinoski attended Boston University and graduated from Antioch College in Yellow Springs, Ohio. He has written more than a hundred books for young adults and children. He is the author of *William Henry Harrison*, *Abraham Lincoln*, and *Rutherford B. Hayes* in the Encyclopedia of Presidents series. Among his recent books are *African Americans in the Visual Arts*; *African Americans in the Performing Arts*; *Bugsy Siegel and the Postwar Boom*; *John Wilkes Booth and the Civil War*; *Marco Polo: To China and Back*; *Francisco Coronado: In Search of the Seven Cities of Gold*; *Nations in Transition: Afghanistan*; *It's My State! Maryland*; *It's My State! Washington*; and *Celebrate the States: Georgia*. He has also written two books on popular music for adults: *The Golden Age of Rock Instrumentals* and *The Golden Age of Novelty Songs*.

Mr. Otfinoski lives in Connecticut with his wife Beverly, a teacher and editor, and their two children, Daniel and Martha. Among his hobbies are reading, traveling, listening to and collecting popular music of the 1950s and 1960s, and playing tennis.